# SHEARSMAN

## 115 & 116

## SUMMER 2018

EDITOR
**TONY FRAZER**

*Shearsman* magazine is published in the United Kingdom by
Shearsman Books Ltd
50 Westons Hill Drive
Emersons Green
BRISTOL    BS16 7DF

*Registered office*: 30-31 St James Place, Mangotsfield, Bristol BS16 9JB
*(this address not for correspondence)*

www.shearsman.com

ISBN 978-1-84861-569-4
ISSN 0260-8049

## Subscriptions and single copies

Current subscriptions – covering two double-issues, each around 100 pages in length
– cost £16 for delivery to U.K. addresses, £18 for the rest of Europe (including the
Republic of Ireland), and £22 for the rest of the world. Longer subscriptions may
be had for a pro-rata higher payment. North American customers will find that
buying single copies from online retailers in the U.S.A. or Canada will be cheaper
than subscribing. This is because airmail postage rates in the U.K. have risen rapidly,
whereas copies of the magazine are printed in the U.S.A. to meet orders from online
retailers there, and thus avoid the transatlantic mail and its onerous costs.

Back issues from n° 63 onwards (uniform with this issue) cost £8.95 / $16 through
retail outlets. Single copies can be ordered for £8.95 direct from the press, post-free
within the U.K., through the Shearsman Books online store, or from bookshops.
Issues of the previous pamphlet-style version of the magazine, from n° 1 to n° 62,
may be had for £3 each, direct from the press, where copies are still available, but
contact us for a quote for a full, or partial, run.

## Submissions

*Shearsman* operates a submissions-window system, whereby submissions may only
be made during the months of March and September, when selections are made for
the October and April issues, respectively. Submissions may be sent by mail or email,
but email attachments are only accepted in PDF form. We aim to respond within 3
months of the window's closure, i.e. all who submit *should* hear by the end of June
or December, although for recent issues we have sometimes taken a month longer.

*This issue has been set in Bembo with titling in Argumentum.*
*The flyleaf is set in Trend Sans.*

# Contents

# Geraldine Clarkson

## Fox, the Prisoner

Fox, the prisoner, impressed on several counts:
1) by offering cranberry and açaí tea in stylish china: conical cups with blue & yellow Clarice-Cliff-like patterns
2) having attended the Station without demur, her apparent lack of need to micturate during a 3-hour recorded session in Interview Room 2
3) her manner of peeing when the occasion arose for her to attend – accompanied – the Station WC: swift, efficient, without noise, gaminess, or a solitary glance into the glass above the basin whilst rinsing her hands (3 pumps on the soap dispenser)
4) the observation that her home had been completely devoid of paper – books, journals, newspapers, jotters, napkins, printing paper, notepaper – with the exception of one lined scrap pinned under a Welsh-Lady paperweight, on which was written the word URGENT and your own contact details.

## Fox, the Prisoner II
*[Editing in]*

2a) her grim intensity when speaking of her ex-lover, his ex-parents and ex-children, the neighbours left, right, and opposite, each one of whom she described in authorial detail; the meat cleaver, the bed-sheets, the lilac bathroom mat, primrose linen shirt – all of which the Polish cleaner was said to have assisted with; and the two fountains of blood, arching, crossing, and seemingly unstoppable, exiting his carotid arteries like the flea-bitten tawny brushes of a vixen and her mate. Crucifox.

# Every Wednesday

was shaped like an avenue of drizzle –
v's pulling away in torqued autumn light –
eager foragers, off, nosing truffle-rich mulch.

An ice pack on my heart to reduce
inflammation, a palmful of pills to slow me
and the girl – who invited her – I don't recall

the start of it – a lolloping lump, her feet hooked
under the sofa – amiable enough, with big
rough opinions which she jutted into our

conversations, without seeming to need a
response, but looking 'knowing', her electric
gaze always switched on. We talked of the dead

but in an easy buttered-fruit-bread
and-tea kind of way, passing the plate.
Except the girl, that is—

she seemed able to remember
the underside of everything, chance
words overheard, signs in the air and

in the breath – queen prophetess of
the sofa, sensing the hop of devils and angels
round the teacups, messages in the leaves – V's

name in a hospital report, in a letter found
at the library and handed to the police, a priest's
subterfuge. The days always ended with some fresh

rush into pain, a yanking from the domestic
into grim medieval scenes, starved vistas
where each of us was alone with hollow cold

and a taunter. The Wednesdays lasted
for a year or so, we don't observe anniversaries
now, and the girl has returned to wherever

she came from, though I see her in shops
sometimes, dragging around a puggish toddler,
whom I recognise as my own, and who'd vanished.

## Beryl-the-Peril Bluebell

Tell blue, flower.
Tell a querulus of best
blue to the flat white
meadow stuck in
picture-book reverie.

Stalk joy with your stem
and your airy, fairy bell.
Stick pistils out
and in that shot-silk thimble
ring like hell.

## Nallybance and the Light Potion

When Nallybance came among us, his sown light – just a trickle at first
onto chipped tongues which winced with the tart unexpectedness
of it – was welcome. We lined up on the second day, Nallybance's
lieutenant having telegraphed instructions. Two spoonfuls for the
sickly kids – straight to the front of the queue. Old ladies with
pendulous stomachs had theirs diluted, and just a single clarified
dose. Not many men were called. There were a few stripling boys,
with archangel faces and bright less-than-beards, who ambled in,
and received huge draughts in ringing silver vessels. The girls mainly
resisted, and by the end of the seventh day he had left us.

## Fool Girl

A scold tale of an Irish Ma,
a bold tale like Brian Boru,
seething with reason and riddled
with sense, an old story, folded
in two, a Sabbath rest
punctured with law and lore,
rolled into a ball to be kicked
by princes to kingdom come.
Charming. Holed-up, giddy
and goldy-locked, she's
sold down the river by dolts.


## Inisnee

Call it Inish-nee, nee, nee, with twelve permutations of Nee in ten
generations, six gorse-humped fields, three starved white beaches
with dozens of deep knock-kneed inlets, and seven headscarved
sisters, living together as seamstresses, unmarried, Conneellys.
Bridgie used to come over from their house by boat for Mass

on the mainland. Now a bridge links the two
and she's stopped practising. Scarlet-sailed hookers cut
the caul of silk water. Weeds stink in the shallows.
No longer making shawls but mending fishing nets and darning
Aran sweaters for tourists, she's started swearing, her mind like a sewer.

# Adam Flint

## Rome

in this print lie traces · soft-soled · of an irritant earth · felt in the
split apart from the welt · wild arum leaves after rain · smeared with
white gore bled from their petals · pure as the curls of bernini's last
christ · cool steep moss-breath · rich from rock-walls · in perpetual
shade · before the touch-burst tamarisk brushes · past arms in light
· acacia blossoming infant fever · byron's sunburnt swim to the
bolivar · the host's unwanted divorce · all other incidents of vigils
neglected · down from teetering minds · pollarded cloud · the
roman pines to a beech-lined tiber · a prison-house for the angels ·
jailed by wings of stone

## In the Fourth Emblem
*(After Nicolas Barnaud Delphinas)*

Part leaves clothing
young bark,

enter divested of
tread in the wood.

Pause, flotant,
at spongy galls – oak-

succubi troubling sleep

strained from the splinter. Lift amid

the ancient,
eyes, to lions.

Their manes sheaves.
Full August.

9

# Untoward Elsewheres

Drowse at the little wood-sheen
the little lit grain brown
fixings splitting their knots

Do not note
the low coals
the slight glows fading

nor the supple textures rawly
courting darkness
over last heat

the trait of meat is pity
the face intact
conceals the head
smiles
at their most beautiful
secure the body's loss

thus wonder dully at
and stifle the affect

       it is a simple plight

to attend what senses serve
or not

       to lean on lances
blank at snow
its fresh shadows thawing
a face in the light of its own

       errancy

is patience, Perceval

the sprent snow winds mould and hone
pricked by keenest carcass
crispens its glitter in the sidling light

the angular warp of gaunt ice
strains violettish
from its gloaming heart

as ingle-wise
the log-moss whiskers
catch
          and phosphoresce

# Mark Weiss

## A Suite of Dances XXIII: No More No Less

You may become of me your own imagining.
The never-ending acquisition and forgetting of language.

When I gave him his first camera
he lined up small things in the beam of sunlight
and studied refraction, translucence,
reflection.

Make much of small victories.

Find the key in the donut.


                    AN DIE MUSIK

                    The dog barks at certain intervals.

I mistook it
for a living thing.

You mount stairs.
You mount horses.
I watch you mount them.


                    FEMME FATALE

                    This graceless child's become
                    a slayer of men.

                    Strong, capable.
                    Nothing etherial about it.

They chatter on about something and she,
her face contorted,
"How can they know,
how can I tell them?"


## THE WANDERING EYE

Touches
his finger tips
with his finger tips.
Over and over. So that's
that. In a sky
that's always
cloudless, fingers
of light, white
fingers, over
and over. So that's
that.

And at the other
end. As if end
lessly, and then.

Enough.
So that's
that.


## THE BONE

Impossible geometry of rocks, the crystalline
          structure writ large.
Fragments
of a mind, one might
have thought,
obdurate. Bone
on flesh.
Bone on bone.

Well then,
it's all
water in the valley,
and one man's daylight
is another's darkness.

Bone on bone.

A life's
tawdriness, a day's
distress. Oh
la.

Here let me say.

Possibly a different understanding of mountains.
It does
as I begin to sleep
have teeth.

Built on a rising figure
there. Damp
quarry
in a damp quarry.

Follow the sound
to the source of sound.

Never asked
the meaning
of it.
Who hasn't faked a rapt
attention?

The meanings
assigned her, an a
greement not to.

Let him
let her
as an act of
not to forget
nor this,
nor that.

Tongue like a cat,
or so imagined.

Plays with the finger where the ring would be, turns
as if turning it. In the midst
of, gathers her hair,
lets fall.

Everyone lives the days of perfect sorrow.

Folded into the number 4
and danced in air.

To the destructive element.

As for instance the ides of
oxides, the where of beware.

Language
as second
speech.
i-di-yum i-di-yum.

Understanding at war
with wonder. Stand
thereunder.
Wandering.

Unease of nudity
as a judgment.

This one long moment
of all we've ever known in a temperate
interval now passing.

We have taught them
to pray
for death.

Rocks
now mute.
Eloquence
in the absence.

Following the accidents of language,
sings in the absence of things.

The best
she she
can be.

Done up
like a butterfly
trussed tressed.

Alights
promiscuously.

We are mountains to those clouds.

Strange, here
in the midst of the desert
of this our lives
to meet a word, but so
it was,
in the wash amidst rocks and cactus
I met a word I'd heard
of
in a different wilderness,
but never seen.

What I know
's the outsides of, as if
another beast.

"Chaos will follow you."

As a fence in a fog,
the dead shout down the living.

Air above as foot treads air.
A breeze, then,
as a set of toes or a rush of rushes.
Look where they bend!
Look where they grow!

This as they were marched to the flames,
substance to sand,
singing.

All of us in the one tunnel.

A cool morning towards the onset of what passes for winter
in Berkeley, the cat stares out the glass door, turns, and asks
to exit. I let her out, and she sits on the porch, staring at yard
and trees, in exactly the pose she'd held indoors. Something
about the rustle and smell.

Store away the particulars of sunlight, a white
blaze across gray
boards, and the shadows of trees and timber. Cat waits
in the midst. Maybe birds.

Birds
to a cat
a form of immanence.

They dance
the quadrants
of the room, to keep

the order
of the kingdom.

Doing figures known from childhood, that
precise, turn at the corner, a hand
raised, but just the one,
and touch the nearest fingertips, then both hands raised
and turn in place.

Such flair
announces who is lord,
who slave.

So, in the larger space
as well, and dance, and dance.

Do you wish me
do you wait for or
attend upon.


## THE GREAT UNSAYING

Autumn.
Into the midst of it.
"Season of..." blather blather blather.


The bird-man cried: "Fowl!"

Faces the door
and meows.

We understand their simple needs.

Wove their *clothing* from girlish lashes.

The rise of diagonals
among these rectangles.

# HOW TO CONVINCE YOU OF MY EARNESTNESS

"Talk 'arf' to the dog."

"Down!" "Oh!" "Come!" "Oh!" "Good dog!"
and howl together.

Arf-hearted conversations.

*This* pretty girl
is like a memory and *that* one
's just a whistle in the dark.


Between indignation and action
compassion may be the seed of policy.

Stone
thrown
strewn
your hair gear hardware
underwear.

Much clearing of throats.

The transcript of happiness.

Language as an act of forgetting. The noun
obliterates the particular.

## SILLY OLD DOG

finds a persimmon
and buries it.


Take oh take your teeth away.

Glass fruit on a winter tree.

Romance of many feet.

Barefoot, she goes
among cats.

Rivers clogged with ashes.

For the summer folks
the sun shines all the time.

But am the man I yam.

Reflection,
as in a puddle.

We all want the winter flower.

Snatches of otherwise forgotten song.


### DISTRACTED

A chord awakens the forest.

Days when I wish for nothing.

In the flowery field the boy says,
"Let us experiment with blindfolds."
"Everywhere we aspire to music,"
he says.

Interrupted by the songs of birds.
"May I charm with all the charms," he says.


Could talk to dogs.
A tilt of the head, and off and running.

He knew what he knew and what he didn't know he knew.

Up there
a wind shapes clouds.

Thin, bent
to herself, twirling
a knot of hair.

## IN PASSING

For a moment
the moon a passport.

Her sinister dexterity.

A stone cloud and a mesh of rain.

## CAROL

1
And Judas sings, oh let us lick your anus lord
oh come oh come to Bethlehem
and let us lick your anus
and let us lick your anus
and let us lick
your anus.

We enact disorder.

Spent a life on tiptoes.

The movement
of a particular body.

Foreswore the beauties.

Let us sustain delight,
discover context.

How to convince them of his hunger.


2
His dusty fidelity.


Parse it.
We mill the wind and water
in the theater of disbelief.

Burnt by autumn,
cuprous light,
love and lust both rampant.

Learned from the birds to dance,
learned to dance
from them.

We pay too much to live in this beautiful place.

Discovery and abandonment of repetitive order.

Shall I invent religion?

Thoughts disconnect from the train of thought.
No comprehension of tastes
without the memory of famine.

The sky was bright
but the road was black
and all the seas ran dry.

The King of Skye.

She thought　He thought
he turned　　she turned
　　　　　　　to stone.

Fresh from the oven.
What could be better?

Cold glint of moonlight.
One fails to acknowledge the presence
of small predators,
or is it,
was even McCoy the real McCoy?

# Harry Guest

## The Satta Pass on the Tôkaidô

                                    up
beyond or else approaching Yui        or
                                        down


The master Hiroshige and his team
drew, carved and coloured all he'd once again
changed from the ordinary to the sublime,
assessing what he'd seen, invented, gauged
along the weary trek to Kyôtô past
inns, castles, cranes in flight, stone lanterns, shrines
mist-wreathed, a temple perching dizzily,
tea houses, watch-towers, rivers crossed on one
thin bridge or sort of ferry under shafts
of rain, at times white flakes from dawn to dusk.
If lucky in the dark you might perceive
a group of foxes glowing strangely round
a nettle-tree as waiting ghosts for their
own god.        A peak, steep either side, comes to
or leads from Edo now called Tôkyô
that east-most  point of civilising life
where daimyô had to turn up now and then
with retinue.        In distance you make out
a rounded pyramid, its cratered top,
some snowlines possibly on the higher flanks.
Nearer and to the right a calm-spread sea,
calm till an archipelago of boulders
causes spray. You watch from here what's called
"a limpid view of the lagoon" where, with
sails billowing, boats dwindle scattering
east-south-east underneath a placid sky.

Faint streaks of tinted cloud stretched by themselves
float half- or more concealed behind Fuji
that almost flawless mountain thought to be
extinct though could be dormant no-one knows
but hopes are rampant still. (We've peered down from
the rim of Asama on seething lava
smelling foul, in Kyûshû looked across
the bay to Sakurajima which smoked
all day while water swaying black between
us and the island steamed.)
                                    That sheer cliff on
the left and almost vertical allows
a narrow path undreamed of years ago
when travellers had to clamber among rocks
along the shore at lower tide and glimpse
up fearfully. Firm pine-trees cling there, ripped
by gales, seem sinister. Above to-day's
path, left, strips of bare rock stand out through thick
low foliage like long blurs of moss. More pines
lean gaunt and ruggèd. Threaten. Wait.
                                    Two males
while wandering down the higher slope pause to
admire the scene to right, their left. The path
soon wending to the frame will vanish to
re-enter further lower where a peasant
climbs, a heavy burden on his back.
He'll also have to leave the print he's on
and halt to catch his breath then chat perhaps
with those down-comers in the hidden part
of that long curling path we'll never see.
This print is Number 17 of all
the stations Hiroshige studied, brought
to life and dazzles us with. Other ones
survive and differ slightly – some have throngs
of trekkers, show one only stretch or tilt
the angle to the sea but what they have
in common is a mostly put aside
phenomenon.

Despite the frequent sun-
or moonlight artists here have never let
a person or a tree throw down across
fields, streets or gardens those flat silhouettes
they actually possess. This is a world
lacking a shadow. On the ground or floor
all stays so clean, uninterrupted by
each still or moving greyish shape, just one
more elongation from the feet or edge
or grip on earth which birches have. You don't
observe that absence, take for granted what
the painter hasn't dwelt with, see a land
not adumbrated like the so-called west
but lit the same way everywhere. Van Gogh
when Japanese prints got so popular
dismissed all shadows for a while and did
his buyers notice? Did we note it here?

## Four

### Trio with Word Sets, Four Each Time

#### OPEN

When days turn dark, each rose, each lily must
feel sun's glow near them fall once, then once more,
even fall back, fade into rays less real
than that pale opal sent to us last June,
why I don't know. Some love cold gems, some don't.

Mist will cast dusk each hour, then near five blur
what keen eyes have seen grow with ease, make murk
seem like grey rain gone thin, dull, very grim.

Soon moon-rise. Slow. When high, yes, a full moon—
that halo held till time will chip each edge
away from that cold disc, then only make

some lone star stir from a dry west into
a wet east and a wind.
                                Then fall. Your rose
that rose some time last year must lose what hues
we've seen, alas know also how a tree
will drop leaf upon leaf, snow come with noon,
fall upon lawn, each step kept soft, pond iced.


## NEXT


That girl with hair like ripe corn goes with calm
past café, shop-wall, bank, shut door. She's felt
they hide what is of idle use, a fake—
some hoax that won't work well till next  good year.

Many like you, I know, envy such hair,
don't talk, look awed. Once a shy poet lost
in no time let a tear fill both fond eyes.

July will turn such hair like hers into
pure gold. Dear girl, whom none must ever name,
stay on if only for a week or so.
Wake up to find a new ring you'd soon wear.


## LAST


All's well. Each cat's safe, in at last. Keep fear
away, don't mind that poor owl's care-worn wail.
Quit this path now. I look over your head
(hers also) see a blue sky fade once Mars
(who's not a star) dips down. We'll try a hymn
Adam sang once, a wry tune to go with
Eve's aria in an Eden they knew that
they must soon walk from, risk some epic deed
life said will last till doom, a day I say
(here I'm an echo only) is to lift

dawn back from dark, make that rare lake we've been
to in a dry year grey with rich pink. Long
ago a lazy swan left here, flew high
from us as if to warn that next year rain
will pour down till each rose, weak also lank,
sees how a lily ages, sags, then dies.

# Julie Maclean

## cause, effect, fish and similes

every night he notes fronts
temperatures     movements of cloud
where the sons reside
sailing miles into the ocean
on the strength of a forecast

not for a moment considering
Lorentz and his chaos theories
kicked about like pig-skin footballs
cumulus forming around his imperfect head like fungus
wind creeping up his imprecise trousers


real weather is a teenager
howling          calculating
its own behaviour
patterns collapse into nebulae of fantasy
like the time I caught one son

cosy in cyberspace examining women
in unlikely but desirable /ferrety/ positions
and my first real lesson to him
within the Theory of Everything —
          *uncertainty     certain*

# A4 Origami Beauty of a Dead Mother

*After an illustration of Alice by Charles Dodgson*

What if we never grow old
or up and instead spend all our time

folding waste paper into planes
paper-bark slivers of papyrus

like skin of the mother
whose virginal breasts surprise

pink-nippled pre-death
and continuing

but in her case premature
Aerodynamic in both hands

missiles whoosh and spin
into night or day

like a diagnosis of your
perfectly balanced right/left brain

DNA of one's exquisite son
paper planes the endgame

folding themselves around curious cells
Extreme training required

to manage serious sport
like rabbit-hole diving

or sketch of a mouse paddling
in two-dimensional stillness towards

a girl with wings and a Roman nose
at odds and evens          fingers and thumbs

# So many girls come to Geelong for a tea party

*After 'Mad house (history painting) no 1'—Sally Smart.*

She's learning so many ways to behave. Living in the mauve. Ignoring crockery airborne and smashed orbiting her special atmosphere. Wearing her house as a hat – a high-rise surprise, curtains billow into crinolines. But that would be so literal, so Gone with the, so Taming of the. What of her natural nurturing of saplings taking root in her apron, lovers migrating in waves across the condos of her face. The way it feels too easy to split her into squares and rectangles of irony and girly significance. One for the Fonda boots. One for the Alice skirt. One for the Hepburn scarf. Belly where the alien grows. One for the gat-toothed smile. One for the Pankhurst hose. One for the rabbit-hole life. One for the Marilyn eyes.

# Batgirl's Night Out on the Town

*After Crystal Precision –Mario Cea, finalist Wildlife Photographer of the Year*

There are no nights
she is too bored or tired

to bounce love songs between trees
the mountain sighs

**someone throws a brick through a window**

but no edge too barbed
to block her resolve

fruit-sick          love-sick          she claims her prize

smashing through sound barriers
barrelling through glass skies

all wings     all eyes     echoes

# James Coghill

## *from* after Aniara

*Harry Martinson's epic science fiction poem*

3

*threaten havoc to our time and state*

peculiar dove / dove of especial note / dove trapped
in a bare white room /
dove that quotes lenin   /   dove that eats grit   /   dove that is
categorically un-pigeon

a new angle of attack reveals     /     unexpected overlap with various

iterations made during a    gunfight    in which your exact opposite

who is the colour
of poached aubergines   /   condenses pre-spatchcocked
on our world's
jolly windscreen / who by some unthought route /

*put   down   exactly   what*

5

( *herewith* *proclaimed* *discovered* )

echo chambers more like iron lungs / that spider tastes of shrimp /
my bedside manner /
the man in front actually donating buttons / buttons the pigeon / a tawdry take
on the art of chagrin /
in the age of spitting / tales of the expectorant ego / how no one really needs
you tonight in crinoline /

never looking quite enough / in all respects / (over coffee) / depleted like a /
come to

think of old isotopes with a delicate sneer / tenderly / the / image of marcuse

bent over a desk /
that one of st jerome / and did he smoke a pipe and if so can he tell me how to /
the hour of the wolf
and all our beloved exercises in imagery          /                    translated
to a series of
controlled detonations / or the exact interpretation of yellow

relict in a tansy / *our ill-fate is now irretrievable*

*my life is in a funny place*

pronounced oh my     /     kettledrum in the carotid
                                        breakneck when
    the greeter    /    I'm in a world of    /    forethought lashed
                                        to a broken clavicle /
    lucy,  when  the  rib   (the dug in rib)  gone  like  a  tick, accidentally,
                                        it's singing
    like gareth c. while  I'm  a  tree  full  of  wasps  overflowing  with  condensed
                                        milk / I suppose


honeysuckle nooses / autotomy of the spirit / fragility so tinglingly (I struck the organist)


neolithic trash makes  /  mola mola eaters  / also fury when every flower is actually


                                        poppies / no-hearted
what I saw was metal frames and feedbags  /  in  grit-filled / dark  as  the  guts
                                        of a microscope,
    and  that  the  worm  is  actually  a  gut  /  creative  intestine  /  comma
                                        under the skin /
        tailbone  /  I wanted  / telling me it told me oysters (a 3rd date)
                                        sweep me round,
            prehensile as love /  embarrass  / my murderous aspect,


                    *come  here  and  touch  it  too*

*grief can shimmer like a phosphorescence*

gelid round a splint sputtering what might be blood or its brighter cousin
suggesting
you've been huffing CO again as if that could be an answer /well it is I suppose /
life and death

of an increment in the post-truth age / tell me again how there's peace in the eye

of the hurricane  / de-extinction of hope / or else a decade spent in the company

of gustave le bon's
proto-fascist yet unexpectedly attractive ghost / herons twitching like triggers
as in the presence
of rivers / you / throw your phone down and stamp on it repeatedly

apoplectic with    /    *death's bitter pill*

# Michael Aiken

## The urge to stare deeply into any body of water...

Rain loosens oil stains on a footpath slick with slime,
awash with unclean, sleepless people.
Streetlights and taxis sail through the storm
as one lone, mangy cat, clumsily desexed, yawls…

A low wind blows. Shuddering, a junkie says
*You feel that? Mother Earth's turning*
*in her shallow grave*

The water draws eels from crevasses;
bricks soften in the old gaol wall
and mortar falls away.
Ibis circle a drunkard, watch
for his wallet to drop.

This is the kind of rain
– undead
walking down the street,
bent against the water –

the rain that draws great eels out
from beneath concrete and trees,
from rifts and fissures in the footpath
to roll like sea lions, following pedestrians.

Translucent bags sluice through grates,
filter across sunlit currents…
…no river known to me –
no river, no lake,
no great ocean not already desecrated
by petroleum rainbows and degraded chains
of molecular aggregates impersonating cnidae.

A stormwater drain:
the concrete remains of one bold water course,
the other reduced to an entombed sewer
left for rats and explorers to haunt;

this city's beloved swamp has been drained for a park
and beneath it, the subterranean train station
now a lake filled with white, blind eels –

Lake St. James – awaiting the disaster,
the apocalypse that will send us under,
seeking shelter in its vaulted rooms,
gathered to supplicate in that flooded chamber
And offer our friends to the predatory hunger
of its patient, anguilline angels.

# Robin Fulton Macpherson

## Sun Through Mist

Normal life has been persuaded
not to be normal.
Colours have been told to calm down.

As if a horizon has stopped
vanishing ahead
and allows us to come up close,
feel the roughness of leaf and stalk
in a lost garden,
hear the half-finished sentences
of the tall people
who sometimes answer, sometimes don't.

## Early Words

«Pirnmill,» perhaps a place-name
like «Shedog» or «Sannox,» jabs
in the flow of adult talk.

«A little-bit-of-bread-and-
no-cheese» — what yellowhammers
chirped swaying on their top twigs.

«Himmler,» «Messerschmitt,» almost
acclimatised, local, like
«double-daisies» and «lupins.»

# Flight-Paths

*Spring sky above German Bight* –
but instead of Constable's
cloud masses, something more like
noughts and crosses in wet ink
spreading, noughts non-circular,
crosses going all spidery

as if Dante's universe
had lost its gravitation
and all the planes, all the rows
of humanity, went pell-
mell everyone his own way
like the scattering of sheep.


# Life-Lines

Revisiting the Tyne
where it meets the sea
(leaving river for sea
or sea for river)
nothing like *hic jacet*
for the distant dead
nothing like street corners
to hold memories

for there's no map of here
no calendar, just
a tumultuous line
soon unturmoiling
back into the tidal
slant of the shallows.

## Evening on Deck

A thin slice of a very new moon –
at last something of substance to watch,
something that knows its place, where to go

unlike the water-coils of our wake
strangling each other, leaving smooth sea;
unlike that ochre cloud, that brush-stroke
jabbed between horizon and zenith;
unlike that fake lighthouse, small window
multiplying the harshness of sunset.


## A Wave

Remembering a good man:

as when an unobtrusive
but not to be hindered wave
arrives from a great distance,

breaks with a whisper along
many miles of sand and smooths
the confusion of footprints

which may be "likened unto"
indecisions, false turnings
and wrongs that can't be righted.

Nothing's denied, but a weight
has now lost its heaviness,
has learnt the buoyancy of

swaying tips of marram grass.

# Alexandra Sashe

## Pastoral
*(Ode to Simplicity)*

Via the Land, via the hours'
fluid awaiting texture,
their unshared and common pace
of the clock, of the embracing landscape

Of the home changing its face
via the sun wrinkles, fields' furrows,
   aging towards its birth

the Song of the tongue resting upon
the objects' silence, muteness, withdrawal, –
  the sole verse of a single word
         sings for
  and out of Love


The wise hands are falling apart,
they sing their fall, and take rest in hay.

The hour touches the land and fills to the brims the cups
of those who were called the last, and came.


## Pastoral

Yet the birds flight
lilac and rose,
       mute and forbidden,
is encountered and received
in the hands
whose embers

are beads of the evening rosary,
whose burns are read in secret
by a child knowing
their fortune.

Patient fingers unfold
their even layers
            of birdly purpose.
    Grains of corn are laid
    for gold, in the hands
    that carry the sun.

Fields' mouth, clothed with obedience,
partakes of the clouds' embrace
and blessing.

It is grass, ever-white with her maiden name,
that belongs to her bridegroom, and
waits at the gate.

## Jn. 12:24

Sow our soil with
a sun-scourged and winnowed grain;
with the gold of your servants
tried in fire; with our binding threads
distilled and converted
into a rain.

Commune once more our soil
with a bread that conveys it
its pure silhouette;
give us to drink from the grain's lot
that never knew its own will.

Teach our eyes to eclipse
their reflection seen in the eyes;

extinguish the luminous of the eyelids,
the self-moon and the self-sun.

Give us an ever-barren land
yielding to our bare feet,
  yielding, for fruit, our even steps
our single hand,
our common footprints.

Transcribe
upon our palms
St. Andrew's greeting, a relic of comfort.

Deny us everything
whereof
we have already been
          weaned.

## Alms

We ask for poverty, we receive its gold,
its warm grass, its nettles and stones.

Each day gives us its day, we walk in
with a soft step, with eyes closed. We see years
                        through its curtain.

Poverty spins us a brown thread
wherewith we are undistinguished from broken
forests. Its song composes our hands,
we lay them still,
they cover our knees.

From the autumn time the pavement inherits
our short walks to the chapel, a muffled footfall,
a flower laid safe in the fog.

At the porch we are mute and let subsist
on our lips
silent articulated letters.


## (Other alms)

Our silent hands are found
good and eager
to make a path

secret and trodden
and loyal
to those
who walk away
from the path-knowing :

bare and unassuming feet
counselled by the grass.


Our eyes see and confess
how bottomless are the hollows
of our hands,
  how sky-blue.
                How clear and warm
is the second water
wherein we dip a milky cloth,

threads unwoven
from our naked
            barren
        denied
    memory.

# Mark Russell

## Men Reading

About war, they say, there is nothing new to hunt. It is as common to write a Dear John letter sitting on the beach at Big Sur, as it is to cycle through the mountains in 45°C. It is the distance between the tongue and the gun, and by equal turns, the veracity of the clinical drugs test, that may land a tornado safely in the desert, far from centres of population. A man found reading Plato in translation in a public toilet may be a Greek scholar after all, or taking precautions. Two men found reading Plato in a public toilet may be understandably annoyed at the intrusion, or the CEOs of rival corporations that produce high performance battery packs for light civilian and military helicopters.

## Men Singing Doo-Wop

About war, they say, there is nothing new to detain us. It is as common for the tenor to be on top, as it is for the bass to be on bottom. It is the chaos of harmony, and by equal turns, the peace of discord, that brings the barbershop to heel. A man insisting on using the off-beat may be passing on his DNA to all and sundry, or about to die by firing squad. Two men insisting on using the off-beat may dress like that on purpose, or to avoid capture by the bad guys.

## Men Who Believe Themselves Caricatures

About war, they say, there is nothing new to describe.

And yet they do. As often as they imitate their fathers.

As frequently as they exaggerate their masculine features.

Even as they are revealed to be of 'least concern' to international conservation experts.

A man may be compared to a hairy woodpecker, or take offence to an ill-judged emoji. Two men compared to hairy woodpeckers are unlikely to be hairy woodpeckers, despite the protestations of literal minded zealots.

## Men Who Believe Themselves

Men in twos may be lining up for more salade Niçoise, or apologising for all the pyromania. A man crying while at the same time laughing may be having trouble composing himself, or dreaming of his days strutting the boards of the South Bank in an all-nude production of Antony and Cleopatra. It is the level of stock in the munitions factory, and by equal turns, the classical structure of a burning city viewed from a far hilltop, that may translate self-pity into wonder. It is the unexceptional. It is the heavily built mundanity. It is the plain-vanilla voracity. It is. About war, they say, there is nothing left to believe.

# Rosanna Licari

## Saudade

During those old subtropical summers
the humidity soared
to an operatic pitch.
We sat on the front porch covered
in a film of sweat
barely moving
unless to sit in front of the fan.
The mango tree stood
like an open-armed goddess
her blessings exposed
as pendulous golden fruit.
The yield that didn't finish up
in a chutney or yoghurt
was foraged by colonies
of screeching bats
and became a fermented compote
under the tree.
The smell rose in the day's heat
to remind us
of bacchanalian rites:
orchards,
young wine,
amorous dancing.
But we were far too sticky
to think seriously of lovemaking.
Then in the afternoon
the clouds bore down
and the storm washed us clean,
as, open-mouthed and facing heaven,
we stood in the drenching rain.

# Archaeopteryx

The puzzle laid out –
fossils examined and re-examined.
Re-image the skeleton.
                                    Re-imagine.
Gradually it came about,
first two legs moving from the pelvis
add bristle and fluff,
then the wishbone, begging for flight.
A demand morphed into wings and
whistled through weightless
hollow bones. Quills added
and a creature marked the transition.
Not all bird –
serrated teeth
a long bony tail
wings sporting claws.

# New Histories

1.

Some poems birth easily. Others don't.
Difficult infants that choose to move,
then stop and keep still. Take a breath,
hold, then push. As with me. Winter.
Christmas Eve in Europe. My mother's
uphill walk on a cobbled street to the
hospital. I held on. She tore inside.

                                2.

                                Now I am more my mother's mother
                                than she is mine. And Africa means

something to her. She says she went to
Addis Ababa. *It's in Ethiopia, you
know?*

The city percolating with war where
her eldest brother, a sailor, delivered
water to Italian soldiers.

Mother then stowed away in a lifeboat
and travelled the continents. *I visited
Australia to feed the lions. No, it
wasn't a dream.*

She gave lectures to the scholars of
Europe and Russia. There were many
things the professors wanted to hear.

*And Rome and Paris, I've been there
before.*

When she was young she stored food in
mountain caves, bartered it and even
gave it to the poor.

*You know I was good to people?*

3.

In the nursing home, Mother collects
cushions from the sitting room and
keeps other people's reading glasses in
her wardrobe and drawers. *They're
mine.* She won't give them back.
Mother shouts and chases people
with her walking stick.

(The nurse tells my brother she'll ask
the doctor about some meds. She then
smiles and says it's time Mother got a
walking frame.)

4.

Her eldest grandson visits often. He's
fourteen and has left home. *But the
others won't talk about this. They
pretend they don't know.* Suggesting he is at school
camp won't counter the
*No! What do you think, I'm mad?*

The talk stops.

5.

Mother sits in her room waiting
for someone to visit.

She cannot recall who.

6.

Prepare for the day
when new histories transform
into no history. The voice on the phone asking:

*Who am I talking to?*
*(It's me, your daughter.)*
*How many children do I have?*
*(Three.)*
*What are their names?*

I recall this as the desk light hisses and flickers
like Mother's brain.

*There's music. Can you hear it?*
*(No.)*
*Who's there with you?*
*(No one. Just me.)*

Be prepared. Tell yourself this
as you stare at your image in the
window.

Kid yourself. It wouldn't be the first time.
Pretend.

Nothing prepares you for this.


7.


Histories weave their threads
through earth and undergrowth.
They die out to begin again
on a wide and ancient volcanic plain.
The wind bends the tall grass
where antelope hide their young.

*My grandchildren are in Africa.*
*They'll come home soon*
to the great southern land
but this long, dark rift is tearing us
apart.

# Mark Goodwin

## This One Water Gesture

from far
off a

river's run s    wirls s    wells
its wet

sounds through

air here holds
a whole

valley in one

vast wobbling
sonic droplet of

place

a sound-recordist first
p    laces her ear

here at

point one at
this place-sized

droplet's edge

her delicate metal
microphone is

not really

solid it is
wet's image of

solidity list
ening now

a recordist m    oves
her ear through

various un
real & real

p    oints towards
river-source un

til her ear her
here-ness zeros

 

                          (cl

        o

                          ses

                         in on)

in on one

      in

                          on

                                   one

ri    p    ple's edge so
wide sounds'

mesh simp

lifies to

to

to

one

impos sible

cryst

al gest

ure

Note: The expression *this one water gesture* was spoken by listener-&-field-recordist-composer Hildegard Westerkamp, whilst being interviewed by composer sound-artist Cathy Lane. (Source: *In The Field, The Art of Field Recording*, Cathy Lane & Angus Carlyle, Uniform Books, 2016.)

# June Emanations, Nantlle Hills, 2017

note: *Cwm Silyn* translates as *spawning lake valley*

I.

Whilst Climbing Outside Edge, The Great Slab, Craig yr Ogof
                    addressed to a reader

Cwm Silyn's three llyns below
– smooth blues slight

ly rippled and spat
tered with the day

-star's sparks

my ropes pale
orange & blue
stripe down

wards across grey tuff

ropes as tugged
map-marks on
actual rockscape

simple linear legends rubbing

their passing over
the complex-crinkled

surface of a
solidified aeon

the day-star's force bounces
off the tuff my skin

seeps salt-wet as

black flies like
letters fallen
from a bible twirl

       two ravens throw
       soft slow *kron-n-n-n-nks* from

       one

              to the o

       ther across
       the simmering cwm

I climb on up
the stone's star-heated
rippled hardness drag

ging my smooth map
-line rope-colours

pitch finished I
anchor to the crag
to bring

up my companion tied
in    to the lines' ends    out
of sight below

and beyond the crag-horizon I've

       just cli
        mbed o
          ver

my mouth gummy
with thick spit
I gaze

-guzzle at the sleek
sky-silent llyns reclined
in the level of

spirits

I almost
believe

I could reach
down and lift and tip
up

a big blue sheet to
pour

a deep bubble of water down
my throat and                          g    guh    guh

glug a llyn dry

swallowing whole its
light & sil
very fish-glinters

                    a sudden high sli

                    ding speckle of dark
                    -spark swallows lets

                    loose gli
                              stening

                    chips of song across
                    the cwm's blue

                    shivering sky-lid

II.

<u>At Summit above Craig Pennant, 734m</u>
unaddressed


      pick

ing steps across light-grey clitter lovely hollow

glug-clun
ks of

      stones rocked

      a geo

logical music folding
an animal's now

ness move
ments in

          to

deep-timed
stone-gong

      sou

           nd

III.

<u>During Return Walk to Road-Head, lower slopes of Garnedd-goch</u>
addressed to my climbing partner & a moor's gone gods

moorland wide-writhing under
sky buzzing white with

the spikes of the day-star

 windless air bend
s into warp
 ing walls

of greased rippling glare

distraught ice-bergs of over
-heated full-fleeced sheep bounce
through black-green reeds away

from us ab
    surd fire
 -faced spectres we

are heat's terror

and it's our
visions that play

on the mind of the June moor

bog-cotton puffs copy
gauzily the flock          are
little sheep stuck
on straws

and heat's fuzz-shine is

a tremor at        at
om magnified
to this

pressed

smudge of

lenticular space this
material of contorted

moor & spook-forms our

extra-real
faces pull all

this moor's molecular
vibrations    its forms

into our skulls a craze

of temperature-rise crystallises
behind our eyes

      suddenly I hear a *gliggle* now
      ribbon-glisten in a narrow channel
      the pebble-bottom pristine through

      limpid prophecy

      we kneel to this
      transparent angel reclining
      amongst the reeds

      we plunge our hands and pull
      up cupfuls and tip

      splashes upon us and

laugh a relief-rapture as a clarity
cold-&-smooth as a home

-coming until now un

known re
-skins our faces with

    flow

    's lo

    ve

# Eluned Jones

## Enlli Child

Speaking in a strange accent, he draws the absence
where one church terminates and another English
replies; comfortable somehow, gentle in his mellow,
cured syllables. His tongue becomes the fingers
that hold this feeling – once, twice – while a sea states
its inconceivable body to a stranger's feet; here,
it says, one man stood on a different ending,
he tasted gorse, heather, those obdurate thickets
that speak sharply of a death. Mine, he queried hesitantly;
then, endowed, it spread deeply as his blood, staying
as the sun moved behind stone and Hywyn's eyes
shaded; for the language that was once a cell
explains itself as lightning, erecting a sanctuary that fails
to refresh the wind, or his fingers as he lingers into wood.

## Shadow language

George Borrow dreamed his shaded English from its parable;
its soaked letters – how it stated a man who is sometimes
called god, but who died here. The precariously mortal body,
it says, was suffused – yes, it suffered and that it bled,
overcome by a symbolism which might have been
his generosity. Strange. My inherited mother tongue shies then
to realise this bodily confession of my own bleeding; but
in your scratched arms, it must say, have you not already
disobeyed; yet how I will cherish the words; and how I write,
unforgiving, this truth among the insular mouths who carved out
a landscape, closing down the stubborn flesh as they did so,
their old man's scalps calling it, futilely, strength.
But why recite the words given aloud to the dead, my English
replies; see, you have made for yourself stone and blindness.

62

## Torn Mint Leaves

It is true that the stems retain themselves
fractionally longer;
for they have a more stubborn flesh

whose sap has dried in resistance around air
to leave a residue, as in blemish or
dirt.

But the leaves are piteous.
Cold, hard words have enunciated the finality
of their structure to a white plate.

My words.
A recessive embroidery arose in the moment
when fingers undercut their first form,

emboldening my page with querulous lines.
But it is the white lines which speak
along my dry fingers.

I did not write this,

I did not write how the one small leaf
is a baby's finger, how it lies
foetal again underneath the dead stem.


## Yellow Flowers

The girl in a black coat
holds two barely yellow flowers.
The flowers are premature, still tightly

wrapped in their own unannounced shape.
I do not know
why she is sitting with her hands

barely containing the never-to-be;
why there is a tense and insignificant
twig on the table

that could have been celebrated
when greenness lifted out, or burst –
vital, voluble – and eyes reached

towards it. My eyes today
see a shrinkage into geometry;
my fingers think of feeling

and encounter only association (death,
transience, the cold tongue of cliché)
and the girl in a black coat

holds two barely yellow flowers
whose supple yet already dead stems
are and will be tightly wrapped.


## Tenderpiece

His empty and burned syllables pique; some salvage
he presumes within the cloying anti-pastoral; skin
automatons expelling old shrillness, those curls
of a sanded grief where Probe knows the deceit
of language – ha!, he laughs his laugh with the texture
of an overripe plum, I shake my hands into the betrayal,
that my eyes disrupt but cause, kissing deeply. Yes,
there may be a lie here, skinning previously benign light
to its needle; but Probe is the quivering in denim surely,
and Mouse is the defectiveness, being required again
to dream in all his little inflamings; the pink lungs
he ventures soul-like, the small nestles of a comfort
he craves within his squall of owned flesh. Alone, he will say,
there are only trees which taper barely into nakedness.

# Caroline Maldonado

## Out of the marshland

*after sculptures by Laurence Edwards*

They are the creek men. Carcass- carriers,
grown out of reeds, forged from
mud, twigs, leaf-litter.

Their lives are mudflats, their history marshland,
tides and sky. From daybreak
to sunset they journey

erect on their raft till they reach their end.
All day they carry our remains
and wear our faces.

★

Today the branches
they carry are huge,
double a man's length.

You can see it in their eyes.

Other days they carry
nothing. Still their
shoulders weigh heavy.

★

The mudflats at dawn
moulded like lava carry
the imprints of feeding birds

65

but sucking the rising tide
are larger holes. Who
has passed before me?

★

Sometimes behind the men
often leading them
(you will see her shadow)
 – the memory-bearer.

From an assembly of bones
her breasts sway
like dry leaves.

Listen to the wind blow through them.

At low tide you can follow
her footprints only so far.

## On our continuing quest for gods

And if they walk out on us one day
with their league-long strides, leaving

this land of herons and silky oyster-catchers,
of wetness and wings, to join a wider world

– if they come across our wayfarers, will they
carry the orphans on their backs?

Look at their faces, battered and smeared
and, for that, human. Let them walk on.

# The next step

Holding tight to his own
morality, sensing that
the gluttony of corpses
in forests beyond the barrows
must stop, he seeks
a new order to follow.

He peers into the intricacies
of roots, their creases
and folds, their under-earth
architecture, and ponders
their complexities but mud
silts his understanding.

One day he'll crumble
and collapse without warning
into an unseemly heap
while from the kiln will step
his twin, fired into bronze,
sleek and shining.

# Jeremy Hooker

## Homage to Charles Reznikoff

There is music
in this man walking.
Alone, he is one
with his kind,
a wanderer between
the old world and the new.
Solitary, in subways
and on sidewalks
he hears the song.
On streets of Manhattan,
by the Hudson River,
from Brooklyn
to Bronx, Bronx
to Brooklyn
and in Central Park,
his day's walk
is his vocation:
listener, composer,
new poet.
ancient scribe,
a wanderer who observes
fellow strangers,
pauses, writes
in his pocketbook
and walks on, unknown,
minstrel at the feast
of common sights.

# Christopher's birds

'there is beauty in birds and all about them'
Christopher Middleton

Man of the sun,
dancer,
whose each step
was, brilliantly,
a surprise,
I could not
write for you
a dirge, or match
your colours
or lore of birds
of foreign climes –
hummingbird
or parrot, condor
or kingbird or loon -
so I call up
an image hoping
it may suffice:
a charm of finches
in a waste
of thistles, which
as they dance
from plant to plant
bring down the sun
with flashes of red,
and black and gold.

# Talking with James Schuyler

Hearing your voice
it's the everyday real
that attracts: so, please,
could we talk? I think
we could have been friends,
so I see us sitting
together in a garden,
on Long Island
or an island off Maine
or West Wight,
some place homely
with summer flowers.
We talk about painters,
your friends or mine,
or John Constable's
'touches of white'
and 'sparkling air'.
Brushstrokes delight,
and quick words,
notations of diarists
we love, Thoreau
and White of Selborne,
Dorothy Wordsworth
teaching her brother
to see, all who, in this
prose age of public ruin
find, or make, 'an image
of life', who know what
we need are small things –
cell, or seed, or word
between friends, so,
please, could we talk?

# Vik Shirley

## *From* The Flotilla and Other Scenarios

*After Lee Harwood*

i

The flotilla ran into trouble about halfway through the procession due to complications associated with the reintroduction of Benzedrine to society. This long-overdue comeback was not, however, being enjoyed by the literary set, as one might expect, considering the associations for which the drug became famous in the 20th century, but instead was being embraced by competitive Sea Captains – or 'Skippers' as they are sometimes known – who simply wished to 'have the edge' and 'make good time.'

ii

"I urge you, Fabio. Say na zdrowie (naz-droh-vee-ay) and keep eye-contact as you knock it back, or else we are done for. Your line about how crinoline hoop skirts were highly flammable and, at times, deadly during the height of their popularity in the mid-to-late 19th century is not going to wash here."

iii

*Sometime in the 1980s. Shopkeeper TONY is stood at the counter while a ten year old stands pointing at penny and half-penny sweets through the glass. TONY is unshaven with matted, greying hair and bloodshot eyes.*

Girl: One of them please.
Tony: Yup.
Girl: And one of them please. Tony: OK.
Girl: And one of them please. Tony: Right you are.

This goes on for some time, until the girl has spent her twenty pence. Behind her, a cortège of girls wait with their twenty pence pieces. Tony thinks about the gin under the counter, the shotgun in the basement and his wife who has recently left him for a more successful newsagent based down at the precinct where Tony can't afford the rates.

iv

"I beseech you, don't do it, Bartholomew. Hurting those who have hurt you only reinforces the original, aforementioned, pain."

v

Of course, later, it was more about the garrotte that spoke volumes (which came in volumes of a voluminous nature) and *Guttersnipe: The Next Generation*. It's going to take a while to get his scent off everything.

# Death Reverie #1

I want my coffin to be covered in artwork by the late ukiyo-e Japanese master, Utagawa Hiroshige.

I want my coffin to have rows of Kokeshi Dolls arranged on top as if posing for a school photograph.

I want my coffin to display a frieze of the sequence of events leading to the inevitable demise of budgerigar keeping.

I want my coffin to have depictions of random 18th century tomfoolery branded onto its exterior.

I want my coffin to have bunting bearing the phrase: 'The more I think about it, the more I resent you' hung from it in a precarious manner.

I want my coffin to stage two relatively unknown Finnish existentialists performing an interpretation of the Mark Rothko painting 'Untitled (Violet, Black, Orange, Yellow on White and Red)' through the medium of dance.

I want my coffin to exhibit miniature models of the cast of axed soap operas from the tail-end of last century and to present them in a way reminiscent of Bosch's *Garden of Earthly Delights.*

I want my coffin to have a film by the fictional art-house director, Jurgen Haabourmaaster, projected upon it. Preferably, his most challenging work. Failing this, Lynch's *Eraserhead* will suffice. Perhaps the scene with the chickens, on a loop.

# Ian Seed

## Ziggurat

1

We love the rolling broadleaf
of your anatomy. Let's hope
the rental suntanned strangers
at a loose end occur
about this silent, new white sofa.
Across the world, wider girls
skipped our sleeve. I had a teacher
knowing it was mine,
gets his first man-bun,
but it's when you see
people start blasting,
I gotta show you the sea.
I want to have it personal
so we can share a nifty coda.

2

You know the feeling
with you right next to me
to put it politely
wolfing the cheeky.
That's the good news.
Let's talk a dark wood
leather bound aesthetic.
There's no better metaphor.
If only I could get to you
before the geese
balance right together,
remote from the sense of sinking
or floating the curve
and dip wander behind them.

3

Their sausages are made from serious.
Their teeth are especially brittle
moneyed light. You need
only clock the punters
salted and sticky mount up.
I mean I have an excuse
render and crisped.
Everything is lubricated.
It feels like good
and subsequent employment
my lips have kissed.
My dad stayed and was, like,
the elephant above Blake's cot
and the can of knotted.

4

Liquid elsewhere items ramp.
Quite a few high street
bits the breath out of me.
Take the pill to your face
and front engine. It's still
quite hinge and bottom
through which Gaspard
the donkey is cannoned.
He has invalided out
enormous guests. Seems like a lark
and a group of apple trees
pimped with my cousin
in a fragrant casket, pink
plump in the empty part.

5

We picked and lost a lovely
pair. Here is the well
familiar barmaid tête de veau
was cattle grazing
those big-eyed chewers.
It wasn't his hand, so why
do we do the things we do
black on white? The shape
of your name
I hope is not a sign
you're offloading. You have a choice,
your space quite brims.
I was invited to its screwing
last week. Unbelievable.

6

How did you and Gaspard meet?
My family itself were the tools
Brexit. My wife can shrink
a French horn, I may add
oversized birds that our father
stitched himself poo head gesturing
so easily one lowers into the ruins
headgear plastic clear streams.
We can expect the cracks
hogged off down the road
their destination plural kissing
decades of bums. There's this duality.
We are the active 86%, and it's not only sweaty.
We found a kind of church in it, you monkey

7

It all adds up, that's the piercing
something of a bumper
franchise if you really want
to amp up the romance.
Spidery is the spark of youth
jostling up a buck backlit,
a good song though not high enough
to look into its face. The sand
coloured chap is as limp
as a dead bird. That's a ziggurat
teetering, and not half
so intimate. We picked at our stump.
It is, hands down,
your first task to mix a cocktail.

# Norman Jope

## In Corleone

Outside the Central Bar, a young man in a ski jacket keeps watch – there's something tucked under his arm. Beside him, a painting of three rustics adorns the bar. Each of them has a sharp unspecified object in the hand. On the other side of the door, there's a poster advertising Il Padrino – a herbal liqueur in a long slim violet bottle. It's almost impossible to see inside or step through that door from here. Only a man in a bottle-green coat and navy jeans, half-obscured, his back to the camera, evades curiosity.

The plasterwork is peeled and venerable and there's a worn-down balcony on every facade. There are very few people about at this time of the morning in the evening, as I glide from street to street on a milk-white vector. Watching for signs of intrigue, I am invisible – unlike the vehicle from which this footage was taken – I am scanning faces that have been thoughtfully blurred so that even the girls, on the poster outside the Solo Gioielli boutique, are as inscrutable as sphinxes.

In this day without a date, at this time without a time, I am unwelcome but nobody knows it – this is a place whose secrets would come at a price. Recalling the hilltop towns I know in England, I imagine the murderous mobs that they might have secreted under conditions of heat and poverty.

At an elevation of 558 metres above sea level, passing a stray brown dog, I exit by way of the Via Spatafora but the road is blocked by the disappearance of my possible route. Perhaps – given all I've seen – it's as well that I'm able to emerge unscathed with a single click of the mouse.

# Three Denouements

*after Werner Herzog*

I'm on the raft, the water is rising and packs of green monkeys are skittering everywhere. My men are either dead or exhausted. My beloved lies, wounded, with glassy eyes and an arrow I don't dare to pluck out. I tell the river that I will escape from this impasse, sail to the far-off kingdom and claim the throne which has always been mine to lose. 'Who is with me?' I ask, knowing that my men are lost and that the monkeys serve their own curiosity and hunger. I can barely take refuge in a fantasy of renewal and triumph, a history that's staged as lesser men stage plays.

Then I'm on the operating table, prone and sodden with invisible water, listening with my feet to the sound of the surgeons explaining me away by the shape of my brain, the imbalance of hemispheres. One takes my brain aside and cuts it up like a cauliflower, isolating elements that came together to make me strange – or attempting to do so. The scribe is so excited at the diagnosis that he decides to walk home just this once, drooling over the beautiful, precise protocol that he will write to define my meaning once and for all.

It's as well, then, that I come to in a merchant's house with furniture one would shudder to sit on in case it cracked. Is it in Wislar, Delft, or Weimar Berlin? Who knows. The important thing is that the rats are still at large and that I am somehow conversant with their language. I open my mouth and smile with a mouth of teeth that could never belong to a passive skull. There's work to be done and, once more, I'm on the dry land of my own ambition.

# Tangerine Dream in the Third Reich

As the Normandy beaches filled with landing craft, another warrior of the Reich was born in the Prussian town of Tilsit. And, despite all predictions to the contrary, the invasion was repelled. Despite the foes that were ranged against it, the Reich prevailed. A thousand-year order was established as the Führer had planned.

Into its silver age, harnessing electronic equipment prepared with sonic attack in mind, the ensemble Tangerine Dream came into being. They claimed that they were named from a line in a long-lost Gothic chronicle, describing the truest shade of the summer dawn. The child of the town of Tilsit, Edgar Froese, led them into musical battle against the recycled forces of the nineteenth century. And, remarkably, prevailed. Their greatest triumph was in 1974, when they played their composition *Phaedra* at the Führer's eighty-fifth birthday concert. And even that lowbrow chicken breeder Himmler applauded, relishing the link between the Fatherland and Classical Greece.

In this parallel world, we cannot imagine what that music would have sounded like. We can only hear music made by another Edgar Froese, another Chris Franke and another Peter Baumann. Music born on the very day that the Europe that made this music possible came into being. Music that seems inconceivable in the absence of freedom.

*Note: Edgar Froese, the driving force behind Tangerine Dream, was born in Tilsit, East Prussia, on D-Day – 6th June 1944.*

# Jennie Osborne

## Breastplate

My breastplate is a series of reproductions
births, over and over, the labour, thrusting forth
of tiny eggs – are they eggs – like pearls
that bivouac on my body
a glistening waistcoat of not-to-be

they cover my ribs like frescoes
in a crypt beneath the asylum where gargoyles
leap and chitter – you know that place
some call it the labyrinth, some
the dream body

they wear little red jackets, like to breakfast
on pearls or anything
small, spherical, precious.

## All the Words I Didn't Say

are buried under this path
   furred over with moss

   but look here's a crack
      and another
            cutting across slant

and what may look like
   grass and buttercup
                up
      thrusting      through

wearing camouflage green
   and pretty soon
      this strip of nubbled grey

            ck
will    bu      le

they'll            break            out

                  air
         into
leap

   shrieking
         cavorting
making
   themselves heard
   in their true colours

   fury-scarlet furnace
   howl-dark well
      of my brea
               king

# juli Jana

## action painting

our round table critique of what is a poem
or what could lead to one
the dissecting & bisecting of ideas

it is a brush stroke exploring
an unknown surface
matching colour upon intent

the words I wanted to say
were not the words I did say
nor were they the ones I wrote
I know I wanted to say something
but it was not yet formulated
therefore I conjured some words

being at a loss as to what to say
I said something that I should not have said
Just because I had to say it
did I

?

# in the cloisters  *sejny*

we enter at the side door
poets with notebooks looking for inspiration
the dim vaulted passage raw with dust
chasings in the walls where electricians
plan to lay cables for light

side passages obliquely
leading to dead ends  empty rooms.
on some walls photographs of nuns with candles
moving in a trance down halls
faces downwards  eyes vacant
others lie prostrate in front of an image
hands outstretched   their tunics flared
in another virgins at an altar being married to the church

we enter the scout room
uniforms  badges  scarves  cups  on display
pictures of monks instructing young boys
they stand limply  their arms at their sides
in a centre room  unrelated objects
gramophones  irons  1960s' TV  wood stoves
next door  some leg irons  whips  handcuffs

on a landing en effigy of jesus with hands of corn
plastic gloves  his photocopied face pasted
in red lentils & barley   blue marbles for eyes
the work of some school project

facing him the virgin mary of paper & cloth covered in bird seed
her rosebud mouth curved with bird seed
a shiny plastic halo dangles from the ceiling
in her stuffed hands a box of goodies

a large sacred room has gold images of the queen of heaven
crown & robe covered in jewels   a row of coat hangers
display embroidered vestments of priests & cardinals

embellished crosses of all sizes   gothic porcelain benches
encrusted flowers  cupids and angels swing from the ceiling

another room filled with wooden crosses
on one a stuffed doll
the tears like blood dripping in crystals

I avoid the next room and the next
hurry down the winding passage looking for an exit

outside some crows call   search for entry

# Kenny Knight

## Last Night

Here on the outskirts
somewhere beneath the stars
on a balcony in the trees
an owl hoots above the car horns,
calling out to welcome the moon
and the mouse that moves
in the shadows.

Your hand touches my fingertips.
The fog lifts a wispy eyebrow
drifting like plankton
across field and lawn.
A rocket that can only dream of space
sparkles over the street lights,
falling unseen like a diluted nightmare.

On the last minute of the year
you flick the head of some dead king
up into the darkness
and close your eyes
counting sheep or cardigans.

Here on the outskirts
the house mumbles to itself
small avalanches of soot and dust
and other rumblings stretch
from room to room.

The wind, indigenous to everywhere
brings a touch of the international
rocking radiowaves across the Atlantic
brings the breath of other lands
to these shores.

The windows chatter away in French.
It is winter now they say
and the sky has grown
as distant as last night's lover.

Here on the outskirts of town
somewhere beneath the ceiling
we slip into sixteen
and wait for the voice
of the owl to call again
a sound as old as midnight,
lovely and haunting
bringing a premonition of sleep
and other delights.

## Making Mary Shelley

I made you
out of bits and pieces
out of this and that
the heart of a frog
the legs of a waitress.

Stuck paper all over your body
tattooed with old words
gave you language
made you multicoloured
added a second coat
a hat and gloves.

Your fingernails
were the colour of a wedding dress.
Your mind a jigsaw of land and sea
Your gaze, filled to the brim
with innocence.

Your body, made out of science fiction
out of superglue and Superman comics,
the shoes of the road,
the face of Mary Shelley.
You were as tall as marijuana
on a night out in the rain.

On Christmas Eve
I wrapped you in gift paper
left you under the tree
sleeping on pine needles
and in the morning
fed you sunflower seeds
filled you with mud from everywhere
rain from a dozen thunderstorms
lashings of spit sprinkled with sawdust.
I taught you to play the piano
to appreciate jazz and Americana.
Gave you a starsign
one slipper in Capricorn
one in Sagittarius
gave you a bicycle pump
the fingers of a short story writer
the eyes of the crowd
cloned you for the supermarket
made you out of the rags of capitalism
made you as durable as vanilla.

## Patrick McGoohan's Care Home

My life in the twentieth century
started in the boardrooms
of Nineteen Fifty One
after winning first prize
in a reincarnation raffle
to be myself.

Somewhere in the years
between the Great Train Robbery
and the sinking of the Torrey Canyon
I set up a neighbourhood tax haven
laundering pocket money
into a piggy bank,
an Edwardian sixpence, here,
a Victorian penny, there,
I was a million miles
and more years away
from becoming
chief clown of the realm,
chief executive of poverty.

In Nineteen Sixty Five
the year I turned fourteen
I became a secret agent
working undercover
on the corridors
of Patrick McGoohan's Care Home,
working as a correspondent
of bicycles and gobstoppers,
working neighbourhood letterboxes
delivering tabloids and broadsheets
seven days a week;
quick as a newsflash.
My life in the past tense
a stick thin bubble-gum chewing
post-war teenage shadow
passing through a world of superpowers.
Cold War print
on the palms of my hands
and the tips of my fingers.

In Nineteen Sixty Five
I discovered a Fleet Street fan club
of fishnet stockings and suspenders
and sermons from kinky vicars.

It wasn't all supermodel
and celebrity junk,
media love stories, fake breakups,
manufactured reconciliations
predictable as the sun
going down in the west,
but with a lot less charm.

My life as a dumper truck driver
started in Nineteen Sixty Nine
on the drying beds of Weston Mill
shovelling shit from all over Plymouth.
The drying beds were flush with tomatoes
at harvest time there was a thriving
black market in Camels Head.
There were rats down there as well
patron saints of the sewers
living on the residue of global capitalism
eating junk food and the leftovers of apple pie.

My life in psychedelia
which might have started
at the Van Dike Club
in the year of the moon landings
the year I became
a stowaway on a spaceship.
An astronaut of acid rock
taking a small step for desert boots
a giant leap for gate-crashers.
I could see the future
and it looked like Eamonn Andrews
waving to my mum from outer space.
My life as a dropout and a beatnik
is one long hallucination
I cannot confirm having flashbacks
of Ken Kesey or the Grateful Dead.

My life as a surveillance camera
panning slightly to the left

of Gus Honeybun
slightly to the right of Derry's Clock.
Working for minimum wage
kitted out in a cheap uniform
reading a second-hand copy
of Nineteen Eighty Four
searching charity shops for a sequel.
Filming on pig farms
on the boulevards of public Hollywoods
looking for the face
of Public Enemy Number Six
finding it on party political posters
in the time of mushroom clouds
and peace signs.

Crossing out names on a family tree.
Crossing out tomorrow in my diary.
Crossing the floor of the orphanage
the radio inside my head
was playing a medley
of Bing Crosby and Bruce Springsteen
when news of my father's death
reached me on Christmas Eve.

In the New Year I made a comeback
made a shopping list for the world
a flea market on Downing Street
a custard pie factory
in the House of Commons
Roy Harper playing McGoohan's Blues
live on the village green.

Mixing with the democratic crowd
on an empire of corridors
snorting capitalism
in a coven of silver spoons
making millions out of fat cat litter
and losing it in the rat race

after investing in Santa Claus.
Making love, making peace with myself
while others were making a living
selling religion for a dollar
or making a bomb making bombs.

My life as a rocket scientist
a scarecrow scaring scaremongers
an old-age pensioner
waiting for Zebedee
taking tea on the lawn.

My life as a part-time
supermarket worker
dropping supermodels
and tabloids in the bin.

My life playing bingo
and backgammon
in a spy ring of lollypop ladies.

My life in the afterlife
of the nuclear family
in a village that cannot be named.


## Molly

For too many nights to number
I have whispered my family name
through this thin wall,
a name as common as Christmas,
have spoken to my mother
have called myself Molly
in the wild seafaring tongue
have dreamed myself
out of the egg

grown feathers and taken
my first steps into the sky.

And now here I am
dipping my beak into the world's
largest rain puddle,
shaking the ocean off my back,
leaving the ground
and the cracked dome
I once called home
to cross the green and the blue
on wings as long
as my grandmother's.

# Du Fu

*translated into Scots & English by* **Brian Holton**

## Drover Toun

1

Reid clouds bourach up wastawa,
Dayset faas owre the level land.
Poutrie keckles inben the wicker yett,
A fremt hame-comer's traivelt a thousan mile.
Wife an bairns dumfounert at A'm here,
The gliff gaed by, they dicht awa their tears.
In a tapsalteerie warld A tholed a gangrel life,
But cam hame in life, chancie tho it wis.
Neibours stow the dyke-heids out,
They're sicherin an sabbin, ilka yin.
I the wee hours o the nicht A lift the caunle:
The twae o's, forenent ilkither, liker a dream.


2

In eild wis A gart ti tak the road,
Hame's no sae muckle blithesome tho.
Browdent bairns winna rise frae their knees,
Feart their faither's for the aff ance mair.
A mind the grand caller air langsyne,
Auld trees that stuid about the stank.
Strang's the souch-souch o the norlan wind,
A hunner hairt-scauds, thinkin on the past.
A lippen on the corns aa bein gaithert in,
An ken the dreep-dreep o the pat-still.
Eneuch for the nou, ti fill lip-fou the tassie:
Fine it'll dae, ti ease the e'enin o ma life.

# Drover Town [1]

## 1

Red clouds heap up in the west,
Sunset falls over the level land.
Poultry cackle behind the wicker gate:
A homecoming stranger has travelled a thousand miles.
Wife and children astonished that I'm here,
Excitement past, they wipe away their tears.
In a world turned upside down I bore the vagrant's life,
But came home alive, chancy though it was.
Neighbours pack the garden wall,
They're sighing and sobbing, every one.
In the wee hours of the night I lift the candle:
The two of us, facing each other, more like a dream.

## 2

In old age was I forced to take the road,
Home's not so very cheerful, though.
Pampered kids won't rise from their knees,
Afraid their father's going away again.
I remember the fine fresh air long ago,
Old trees that stood around the pond.
Strong's the sough of the north wind,
A hundred sorrows, thinking about the past.
I'm relying on the grains being gathered in,
And know the drip-drip of the pot-still.
Enough for now, to fill the bowl brim-full:
It'll do fine, to ease the evening of my life.

## 3

A paircel o hens skirlin an skellochin –
Guests come, wi the hens aa fechtin, tae.
Yince A'd chased the hens inti the tree,
A heard the chappin on ma wicker yett.
It's fower or five auld yins that's here
Ti speir about ma lang an ferawa traivels.
In ilka haun a wee bit something brocht,
The whisky pig's cowpit, it's drumlie, then fine:
"Och, dinna nay-say a dram, wersh tho it be:
There's nane ti plou our fields o corn.
War an fechtin, an aye wi nae devaul:
Our laddies taen, ilkane, eastawa ti the airmy."
"Allou me nou ti gie ye a sang, auld yins,
Sic hership maks ma hairt owre great, A vou".
The sang dune, we leukt ti Heiven wi a souch,
Ilka haffet begrutten wi our tears.

3

A parcel of hens skirling and screeching –
Guests have come, with the hens quarrelling, too.
Once I'd chased the hens into the tree,
I heard the knocking at ma wicker gate.
It's four or five elders that are here
To ask about my long and faraway travels.
In every hand a little something brought,
The whisky jar's tipped, muddy, then fine:
"Oh, don't turn down a dram, insipid though it be:
There's none to plough our fields of corn.
War and fighting, never an end to it:
Our lads taken every one, east to the army."
"Allow me now to give you a song, elders,
Such hardship makes my heart too full, I vow".
The song over, we looked to Heaven with a sigh,
Every cheek stained with our tears.

Note
[1] 羌村: 羌 Qiāng is the name of a Tibeto-Burman speaking people who still
live in western China. Etymologically, the name seems to mean something
like 'sheep herders', hence my translation.

# Tania Hershman

## The Laughing Bottle

*a prose sonnet*

Thirty a day and enough gin. I make my way down to the shops for tonic. Ice I have, and I keep buying more in. I sit and drink and it's never enough.

I switch to whisky, find a favourite single malt. The programmes on the television buzz and I close my eyes. Missing you will be something that is not my fault. Missing you is loud and quiet and sly.

When you arrive you want red wine. I put away the whisky and watch your hands. We sit with Merlot and we stop time. The television dies and I throw it out.

You leave and never leave and leave again. Our endless game.

# Notes on Contributors

MICHAEL AIKEN lives in Sydney, Australia. His first book, *A Vicious Example*, (Grand Parade Poets, 2014) was shortlisted for the NSW Premier's Kenneth Slessor Prize for Poetry, the Dame Mary Gilmore Prize and an Australian Book Design Award. In 2016 he was selected by David Malouf as the recipient of the *Australian Book Review*'s inaugural Laureate's Fellowship, for which he wrote the book-length poem 'Satan Repentant'.

GERALDINE CLARKSON has two chapbooks to her name: *Declare*, from Shearsman Books (2016), which was a Poetry Book Society pamphlet choice; and *Dora Incites the Sea-Scribbler to Lament* (smith | doorstop, 2016), a Laureate's Choice pamphlet. A third, *No. 25*, will appear from Shearsman in 2018. She is currently working on her first full-length collection.

JAMES COGHILL is an ecopoet with an abiding interest in lyric sequences, Swedish culture, and animal studies. He has had poems published in *The Rialto*, *Lighthouse*, and in anthologies from Sidekick Books. Currently residing in Greenwich, he sometimes blogs at thesolenette.wordpress.com .

DU FU (712-770) is one of the greatest of all Chinese poets, and though he was high-born – he was a distant, poor relative of the Imperial family – his career was not a glorious one, and he was more than once seconded to junior posts in remote regions, or stranded by rebellions and border wars. He knew the meaning of sorrow and grief – one of his children died of hunger during a prolonged absence – but transmuted this personal pain into hauntingly beautiful verse of great grandeur and complexity, poetry which is wittily innovative, and almost impudently virtuosic. Though written with impressive technical bravura, many of his poems are like short, heartrendingly sad jokes.

ADAM FLINT lives in Berlin. Previous poems have appeared in *Stand*, *Blackbox Manifold*, *Shearsman*, *Corbel Stone Press: Contemporary Poetry Series*, among others.

ROBIN FULTON MACPHERSON is a Scottish poet long resident in Norway. His translations of Norwegian and Swedish poets have been widely published, and his own *A Northern Habitat: Collected Poems 1960-2010*, was published by Marick Press in the USA.

MARK GOODWIN's most recent publications are a chapbook, *All Space Away and In* (2017), and a full collection, *House At Out* (2015), both from Shearsman Books.

HARRY GUEST has recently published a collection of his translations, *Otherlands*, with Shearsman (2017). His poetry has mostly been published by Anvil Press Poetry (now owned by Carcanet), in the volumes *A Puzzling Harvest* (Collected Poems, 2002) and *Some Time* (2010).

**TANIA HERSHMAN**'s debut poetry collection, *Terms & Conditions*, is published by Nine Arches Press, and her third short story collection, *Some Of Us Glow More Than Others*, by Unthank Books. Tania is also the author of a poetry chapbook, *Nothing Here Is Wild, Everything Is Open*, and two short story collections, *My Mother Was An Upright Piano*, and *The White Road and Other Stories*, and co-author of *Writing Short Stories: A Writers' & Artists' Companion* (Bloomsbury, 2014). Tania is curator of the short-story hub ShortStops (www.shortstops.info), celebrating short-story activity across the UK & Ireland, and has a PhD in creative writing inspired by particle physics. Hear her read her work on https://soundcloud.com/taniahershman and find out more here: www.taniahershman.com

**BRIAN HOLTON**'s *Staunin Ma Lane – Chinese Classical Poetry in Scots and English* was published by Shearsman Books in 2016. He is widely published as a translator, and his recent translation of Yang Lian's *Narrative Poem* was a Poetry Book Society Recommended Translation. He has published a dozen books of translations of the poetry of Yang Lian, as well as many classical and modern poems and short stories, and the novel, *Paper Cuts*, by Leung Ping Kwan.

**JEREMY HOOKER**'s diaries and journals are published by Shearsman, as is his most recent collection, *Ancestral Lines* (2016). His collected poems, *The Cut of Light: Poems 1965-2005* was published by Enitharmon in 2006. He lives in South Wales.

**JULI JANA** lives in London and is the author of a Shearsman chapbook, *r-a-t* (2014).

**ELUNED JONES** lives in Aberystwyth, Wales. She has Masters degrees in 17th-century English Literature and Archives Administration and currently works as a civil servant for the Welsh Government. A fluent Welsh speaker, she currently writes mainly in English. Her poetry has previously appeared in *Shearsman*, as well as in *Envoi, The Interpreter's House* and *Ink Sweat and Tears,* among others.

**NORMAN JOPE** is the authors of several collections, including *Dreams of the Caucasus* (Shearsman 2010). He lives in Plymouth.

**KENNY KNIGHT** lives in Plymouth and has two collections from Shearsman, most recently *A Long Weekend on the Sofa* (2016).

**ROSANNA LICARI** is an Australian poet and writer. She is the poetry editor of online literary journal *StylusLit* ( www.styluslit.com ).

**JULIE MACLEAN** lives in Australia. She is the author of *Lips that Did* (Dancing Girl Press, USA, 2017), *To Have To Follow* (Indigo Dreams, 2016), *Kiss of the*

*Viking* (Poetry Salzburg, 2014) and *When I saw Jimi* (Indigo Dreams, 2013). website: www.juliemacleanwriter.com

**CAROLINE MALDONADO** is a poet and translator whose poems have appeared in anthologies and in magazines including *Tears in the Fence, Long Poem Magazine* and *Poetry Salzburg Review*. Her publications include co-translations with Allen Prowle of poems by the Italian poet, Rocco Scotellaro, *Your call keeps us awake* (Smokestack Books 2013), a pamphlet, *what they say in Avenale* (Indigo Dreams Publishing 2014) and the forthcoming *Isabella* (Smokestack Books 2019). Photos of Laurence Edwards' sculptures can be found at http://laurenceedwardssculpture.com/

**JENNIE OSBORNE** lives in Devon and has two collections from Oversteps Books, *How to Be Naked* and *Colouring Outside the Lines*.

**MARK RUSSELL**'s most recent works have been *Shopping for Punks* (Hesterglock Press), and *Spearmint & Rescue* (Pindrop). Other poems have appeared in *Tears in the Fence, Molly Bloom, Butcher's Dog*, and elsewhere.

**ALEXANDRA SASHE** lives in Vienna. Shearsman published her first collection, *Antibodies*, in 2013, and will publish her second, *Convalescence Dance* in 2018.

**IAN SEED**'s collections from Shearsman are *New York Hotel* (2018), *Identity Papers, Makers of Empty Dreams, Shifting Registers* and *Anonymous Intruder*.

**VIK SHIRLEY** is a poet from Bristol, whose work has appeared in *Stride Magazine, Zarf Poetry, Hermeneutic Chaos Literary Journal, Lunar Poetry* and *Ink, Sweat and Tears*. She is currently on the Creative Writing MA at Bath Spa University. Previously Vik has written and recorded music as one half of an electronic duo, Canola Tenderfoot, with albums released on Malicious Damage and Slime recordings.

**MARK WEISS** has published four major collections, the most recent being *As Luck Would Have It* (Shearsman Books, 2015). He has also edited anthologies of Mexican and Cuban poetry and translated several books of poems from Spanish, including Gaspar Orozco's *Book of the Peony* (Shearsman, 2017).

www.ingramcontent.com/pod-product-compliance
Lightning Source LLC
Chambersburg PA
CBHW030959090426
42737CB00007B/609